On Ma[illegible] as Vocation

Dave Leal

Lecturer in Philosophy, Merton College, Oxford

GROVE BOOKS LIMITED

RIDLEY HALL RD CAMBRIDGE CB3 9HU

Contents

Preface

My initial motivation in writing this booklet arose from concern over two trends. One concerns an attitude towards the extent of individual freedom in relationships. This attitude shows itself most clearly in the rise of cohabitation as an alternative to marriage, and also shows itself amongst those who *do* marry in an easy acceptance of divorce. This particular trend is most clearly the target of chapter 3. The other trend is a kind of abstracted idolatry of marriage which fails to see the need to demonstrate the actual significance of marriage for human lives and relationships. This is one target of chapter 1. I hope, though, that readers will find in the booklet something more constructive too!

I wish to express thanks to those who have helped in the preparation, especially to David Attwood, who provided detailed comments and many helpful suggestions. The booklet undoubtedly owes any intelligibility it now possesses to the comments of such friends, and I am enormously grateful. Of course, anyone thinking and writing about marriage will be influenced not just by other writers, but also by the example of friends and family. Most of all, in the sharing which has taught me from experience of the good there is in marriage, I must mention Clare, my wife—not just in thanks to her, but thankful also for the calling which we live out together. May others know in their lives the same joy in their callings.

The Cover Illustration is by Peter Ashton

First Impression January 1996
ISSN 0951-2659
ISBN 1 85174 308 1

1
What's the Good of Marriage? Two Approaches

There are two general investigations to be undertaken into the nature and significance of marriage. One is to look at the goods of marriage viewed *externally*, as it contributes to society and thus as it concerns those who exercise political and social influence. The other is the *internal* character of marriage as experienced by the couple. The latter is our concern in this essay. It could well be argued that in the inherited categories of theological discussion this topic belongs more to pastoral thinking than to moral. Against this is firstly that the discussion is not about some one particular marriage but about *each* marriage, and about this form of human life taken in a quite general way. Secondly, if the discussion of the legitimacy of divorce *is* a question for moral theologians, anything which can throw light on the nature of each particular marriage is bound to be of relevance for moral theology. So we cannot avoid regarding this internal aspect as part of the specifically moral theology of marriage.

External Goods

We begin by separating out these two areas of 'external' and 'internal.' There has actually been a great deal of discussion of the 'external' goods of marriage recently. In the month that this booklet was written, for example, a book has been published which collects together a number of essays related to the theme of marriage.[1] It carries a declaration on its cover that,

> 'There is no society known to history or anthropology whose social order has not been based on marriage. The universal deployment of a binding contract to control reproduction and child-rearing reflects wide understanding that societies which lack cohesion cannot survive long.'

It is not clear whether this is making two points or just one in favour of marriage—whether, that is, in addition to the contribution of marriage to child-rearing there is a *separate* contribution which it makes to social cohesion and social order. In any event, arguments in favour of marriage along these lines are very unlikely to have any direct, practical effect on couples who are contemplating either marriage or divorce. Just thinking about the welfare of children, it is surely likely that those couples for whom their children *are* a significant consideration will already have taken them into account to some degree in their decision. If the welfare of their children is *not* a significant consideration for them, it is sadly implausible to think that a reminder of it would be enough to alter their decision.

1 Robert Whelan (ed), *Just a Piece of Paper?* (London: IEA Health and Welfare Unit, July 1995).

Secondly, if social cohesion were a reason to *encourage* marriages, it would nevertheless be a strange couple who married *in order* to promote social cohesion, or who failed to go through with a contemplated divorce simply on the grounds that their behaviour would have a negative effect on society generally. It is possible that overall social cohesion might survive just a very few divorces intact. But if divorce is already common in society it may seem hardly likely that one more specific divorce will represent a significant *additional* strain on that cohesion.

A significant feature of this discussion of *external* goods is that it is aimed at policy makers and social analysts rather than at helping individuals and couples to understand the nature and purpose of marriage better.[2] However, if divorce is in itself bad, if cohabitation should not be recommended above traditional patterns of marriage, if (above all) marriage is to be seen as a positive good and something to be hoped for and cherished, it will not be these 'external' considerations that will make the difference to the people who actually contemplate marrying.

Internal Goods

None of this is meant to suggest that books and discussions such as those referred to are without value. They need to be supplemented, though, with an honest assessment of the *internal* goods of marriage. Christian literature contains many such treatments, though it seems that much of the modern material on marriage has appeared negative, concerned more with counteracting a rising acceptance of divorce, perhaps aimed more at legislators. The traditional lists of *internal* goods (for example: procreation and the formation of children in the Christian life; the faithfulness of each partner to the other; and the symbolism which the permanence of their union offers of the union of Christ and the church) may inspire the Christian, but are by no means all likely to commend themselves to those outside the churches.

The more secularist interpretation found in the marriage service of the Church of England's *Alternative Service Book* (companionship, sexual relations, children) might well seem intuitively to be 'good things' to a much wider audience. A couple might, though, reject the possibility of children (or, indeed, be amongst those which the *Book of Common Prayer* terms 'past child-bearing'). Or they might regard their companionship as a continuing voluntary commitment each to the other. (We might add that with sexual relations outside marriage being absolutely normal, thinking of sexual relations as a *particular* good of marriage would scarcely appear credible.) It might be far from obvious *how* anyone might use these particular 'goods' as an apologetic for marriage, as a set of reasons to marry.

2 As an illustration: 'The point [of a discussion of 'family values'] is simply that the conventional family unit is an efficient mechanism for combining bringing up children and earning a living. One does not need to call for a return to the extended family to acknowledge that single parenthood and divorce make people, and countries, poor.' Hamish McRae, *The World in 2020* (London: HarperCollins, 1994) p 43f.

The following passage sums up one particular understanding of entering into marriage which has been exhibited by some parts of the church:

> '...Each marriage, in so far as it is a conjugal union between a particular man and a particular woman, arises solely out of a free consent of the two partners; and this free act by which each yields and receives the specifically marital right is so necessary for the constitution of marriage that it cannot be supplied by any human power. But the only rôle of this human freedom is to decide that each of the partners wishes in fact to enter the state of matrimony, and to marry this particular person. The freedom of man has no power whatever over the nature of matrimony itself, and, therefore, when once a person has contracted marriage, he becomes subject to its essential laws and properties...'[3]

The essential elements to note here are the importance given to consent, freedom, and the idea of 'the nature of matrimony itself,' with 'its essential laws and properties.' There is behind such words a belief which we might express by saying that marriage as a concept has a particular form and shape independently of any actually existing marriage. Imagine for example that I agree with a particular woman that it would be good for us to marry. We both do so absolutely voluntarily, and give our consent to each other. From that moment onwards our freedom has been bound into an institution from which 'escape' is not possible—we might almost say, not *logically* possible, because if it really *is* capable of being 'voted out of,' it cannot have been a marriage.[4]

Marriage and Human Living

Should we believe that there really *is* such a 'thing' as marriage over and above the existence of actual human beings, and that it is a form of human existence to which those who choose it are in some sense morally committed to conform? This raises all sorts of fundamental questions regarding the nature of morality and of obligation. Perhaps to the religious mind it implies a preexisting conception or idea of marriage, maybe within the mind of God, with human

3 Pope Pius XI, Encyclical Letter *Casti Connubii* (1930). From J. Neuner/J. Dupuis, *The Christian Faith* (New York: Alba House, 1990) 1825 [Denzinger-Schönmetzer 3701].

4 An amusing tongue-in-cheek illustration of this position was given in a recent journal article (Christopher Wolfe, 'The Marriage of Your Choice' in *First Things* 50 (February 1995) pp 37-41). The writer asks: why, if our society is so liberal in its tolerance of a wide range of views on relationships and social structures, is it not possible to request the law to *enforce* the expressed wish of two citizens to marry for life, so that, if one of them later wished to 'escape' the marriage, the law would prevent it? The background to this question is an investigation into the practical and logical limits of liberalism. To the present author, the article raised another point: is it helpful, sensible or even quite truthful to regard the Christian view of marriage as a kind of life-sentence in this way? That—a 'sentence'—is clearly how the average secular reader might be expected to read the suggestion of an absolutely irrevocable lifelong marriage; an open-ended commitment to an unknown future with a voluntary rejection, *in advance*, of the *possibility* of any 'let-out-clause.'

beings created so as to conform to this pattern or order, this 'nature of matrimony itself.' This, though, is pretty unsatisfactory. It is not unsatisfactory because of the talk of 'forms' or 'orders' of human existence as such, but because of the *priority* which this form of human existence appears to have over the existence of human beings. We might say in response that there is no such thing as marriage apart from actually existing human beings.

In saying this we might remind ourselves that Eve's creation in Genesis 2 is designed to fulfil a particular need in Adam's life; to overcome his loneliness, a suitable companion is made for Adam. Perhaps this account hints that there might be reason to take companionship as a *primary* good amongst the 'internal' goods of marriage.[5] But be that as it may, it certainly suggests the simultaneous conforming of marriage to human need alongside the creation of human beings. If human beings are to be true to the demands of an abstract 'concept of marriage,' then it will be because it is good for them—amongst other things, that is, because 'it is not good for man to be alone.' The 'form of marriage' to which the marrying couple are said to be committed by their free consent is actually a form *implicit in the kind of thing which they are as human beings,* male and female, and in the kinds of lives which can offer them fulfilment.

One might remember Jesus' insistence that 'the sabbath was made for humankind, and not humankind for the sabbath' (Mk 2.27), and suppose that there is a parallel here with marriage. The only qualification we might need to make is that the purpose of each of these contributions to human well-being have to be assessed on their own terms. From the correct observation that the sabbath laws can be placed under a general concern for human interests, it does not immediately follow that they can be broken unthinkingly whenever human desires conflict with them. With marriage likewise. We ought not to regard divorce as freely available just because people apparently want it, or think that superficial human desires can automatically override what is in fact in the deepest human interest—in the interest, that is, not *just* of 'society as a whole,' but of the couple themselves. Whether divorce might, from this perspective, *ever* legitimately be made available to a married couple is obviously of vital importance for the development of a full Christian theology of marriage. The bearing of the 'hardness of human hearts' upon this is far from clear. It focuses on the extent to which divorce is a more ultimate admission of failure and irredeemability than any Christian ought properly to make.

It is worth pointing out explicitly something that has been implicit in everything which has been said so far. We are concerned with *marriage,* and not with

5 And the creation account in Genesis 1, which stresses 'the image and likeness of God' in the making of male and female, stresses another internal good, one version of the 'iconic' good of marriage; here as a symbol of the Godhead rather than as a symbol of the relation of Christ and the church. Thus these two creation accounts might each be said to exhibit one of the *primary* internal goods of marriage (Compare Karl Barth, *Church Dogmatics* III.2 (Edinburgh: T&T Clark, 1960) §45.3). The good of procreation appears rather to be enjoined *upon* their relationship, and recognized as obedience. We may term this a *secondary* internal good.

some special phenomenon called *Christian* marriage. Certainly, we are asking questions about marriage from a Christian perspective; so, for example, the conception of human well-being by which we should seek to justify marriage would be a Christian conception. We might expect Christians to be more willing to submit to this understanding of human well-being than others, of course! The sort of understanding we might have in mind would include features such as that the worth of my life is much more than the sum of my present and immediately prospective pleasures, and that the good of my life depends crucially on my willingness to lay it down. It might even be that the vision of human well-being which Christians have is *so* far from anything which a non-Christian could share that no-one outside the Christian faith could find support for marriage intelligible on this basis. Even *that* result of the investigation would surely be worth the effort, even if only as one component of a proper understanding of the proclamation of the gospel.

Called to Marriage?

It appears that in our relationships we are called to *some* state within the norms of human life which present themselves in the area of marriage. The questions which might most obviously be asked regard the conception of 'being called to' which is operating here, and the range of things which might be counted as 'norms of human life.' This last question seems to be part at least of the point of Matthew 19.3-12, where Jesus narrows to a vanishing point the range of options available between celibacy on the one hand and a rigorous conception of lifelong marriage on the other. We may be called to be celibate, or to be married.

The exact nature of this 'calling' is a question that will concern us through the rest of this booklet. In the quotation about the entry into marriage (page 5) there was every suggestion that human beings are free to choose marriage, but not free to alter the kind of thing that marriage is. They are free to give their consent to a partner, but not free to be released from this marriage at some later date, except by death. Within this pattern there are said to be *two* freedoms: to choose marriage; and to choose (insofar as the other is willing) one's partner.

There has recently been some controversy regarding whether celibacy can be enforced on a person by a human order. The claim is made that celibacy is a specific calling, *accompanied by the appropriate gifts of God* to enable this to be a fulfilled human life. But for marriage, too, we may ask whether matters can be seen in this light. Is marriage, seen in the light of the claim that 'the free act by which each yields and receives…is so necessary for the constitution of marriage that it *cannot be supplied by any human power*'[6] (an admittedly ambiguous phrase), a special calling, a calling not just to the married state, but even to marriage to this one particular person? To accept this would be to dramatically alter our perception of freedom in relation to marriage—to view marriage as vocation.

6 Pope Pius XI, Encyclical Letter *Casti Connubii*, emphasis added.

2

Making a Marriage: 'That which God has Joined Together…'

The issue of consent has already been mentioned, and it is a good place to begin the next part of our discussion, because it raises the question of the meaning of marriage in the most acute way. It is no accident, though it might escape a casual glance, that the word used is 'consent' and not 'choice.' For a start, of course, I can only marry a person who is *willing* to marry me. I cannot ultimately just *choose* to marry anyone, because I do not have the authority over that person to *compel* marriage to me. For this reason, no individual can have any 'right' to marriage. So, then, we speak not of 'choice' but of 'consent'; but to what is this consent given? A first attempt at an answer might be: to the fulfilment of the desire of the other person to marry *me*. Two individuals each wish to be married to the other, and they each consent to the other person's desire, allow the other to have his or her desire.

The concern to ensure consent finds an obvious expression in our marriage services, where each of the couple are asked independently 'Will you take…?'; without this consent there can be no marriage. And what *more* is needed, beyond consent? Vows are exchanged, which have the functions both of making promises each to the other and confirming to the gathered witnesses their understanding of the marriage into which they are entering. It is natural to suppose that the couple themselves are the significant actors here and that by their actions they are the makers of their own marriage. This indeed has become something of a normal theological view. It is explicit, for example, in Helen Oppenheimer's book *Marriage*, when she discusses the sacramentality of marriage and states that 'it is the couple themselves who are the ministers of this sacrament.'[7]

God as Minister

Apart from the obvious issues regarding the nature of sacramentality, the important question to ask here is what '*minister* of the sacrament' implies. It may be a mere slip when the next sentence in the book reads, 'A marriage is made, legally and theologically, by a man and a woman solemnly consenting to take each other for life.' Read with charity this may be fine; but just as *legally* marriage might be said to be more than just this solemn consent, so *theologically* we might ask whether more is required than has been expressed here so far. It is worth reflecting on some words of Christ which have a fairly significant place

7 Helen Oppenheimer, *Marriage* (London: Mowbrays, 1990) p 64.

in our marriage services: 'that which God has joined together, let no one divide.' The words are used as the couple are 'held together' by the minister, and they appear to be used with reference to the couple.

Perhaps the use of these words is intended to constitute a reminder to the congregation of the inviolability of the marriage bond 'as such.' It is then simply a solemn general pronouncement of God's stand against *divorce*. However, the puzzling words 'that which *God* has joined' might give us pause for thought. One might actually hear the words in a quite natural way as implying a specific act of God in the joining of this particular couple. The words of the service then serve not simply as a general reminder of 'the sanctity of marriage as such'—to those who hear the resonance of the Gospels in them they will *at least* do that, serving as a reinforcement of the message that Jesus affirmed the inviolability of marriage in God's intention—but as a quite particular claim regarding this *specific* marriage, namely that *God* has joined *this* couple in marriage. We may be quite properly curious to ask if this is at all a plausible hearing of the words, and, if so, whether we can go on regarding the couple themselves as the 'ministers of the sacrament.'

If we *do* so regard them, it is perhaps because we *identify* their desires and their consent as *coincident* with God's joining of them. In other words, we develop a view of providence which allows us to use the language of divine action for what will have been for each couple a story that could be told in quite different terms. God's action in joining them actually *is* on such a view expressed in the experience of love and desire each has for the other. This is not necessarily to be seen merely as euphemism, though it will obviously threaten to collapse into euphemism. On this view, it appears impossible to imagine as anything but an error or a joke the question whether the couple might marry against God's will—whether, that is, their 'marrying' might actually *not* be an instance of God's joining of them. The issue here is not whether the couple's attempt to marry is defective in one or another of the range of impediments which might be cited (such as one of them attempting bigamy). It is rather whether there is anything at all *over and above* their consent and perhaps their vows, *all normal human impediments being safely discounted*, the absence of which might count against the validity of the marriage.

Marrying against God's Will?

Obviously, to raise this question at all is to focus our attention very directly upon the *Christian* interpretation of the marriage which has taken place. From the *legal* standpoint, a marriage quite certainly exists, and any objection to it on the grounds of a belief that somehow *God's* consent is not present would be treated with incomprehension. Yet it is clearly possible that of those many marriages which *do* end in divorce a great many have failed not merely through subsequent human wickedness, stupidity, or hardness of heart when everything seemed destined for success, but appeared profoundly ill-advised in the first instance. Where the love and desire experienced in other marriages has appeared to be a sign of God's action in bringing the couple together, in this or that marriage we see the love and desire as obsessive, unhealthy, not godly at all.

A great deal of the thinking which *is* done in preparation for marriage in Britain is undoubtedly done in the churches. Yet a great many churches may appear, at least to those who come to be married in them, as simply another agency with a function to be performed at their request. The focus on consent as a virtual final word in the making of the marriage may actually underline this view, and make them unwilling or unable to hear any counsel which they are offered.

To any minister who has been faced with the prospect of marrying a couple where everything seems in order, *except* that there remains a kind of nagging prayerful unease on his part, these thoughts will not be new ones. There was a recent correspondence in the papers regarding the rights of a minister to conscientiously object to performing a marriage service for a couple who request one. The case was, as I recall, one of a cohabiting couple, but the specifics matter less here than the interest of the general principle. There can be a perfectly human element to this, a gut-level hunch that things are unlikely to turn out well. And yet equally we are aware that these hunches and predictions can turn out to be quite gloriously false. The most prospectively implausible marriages have turned out to be not simply tolerable for the couple, but to offer an example of love which fulfils for those who know them a good measure of the 'iconic' good of marriage.

We *might* say that because nothing is certain, and our best predictions can turn out to be so wrong, the balance of the judgment (almost the 'benefit of the doubt') should go to the desires of the couple themselves. There might well be cases where a genuine doubt exists regarding the consent of one of the couple, or even of both of them when pressure is brought to bear by others. But wherever proper consent *is* believed present on both sides we might say that no human authority external to that couple should have the power to override it. The apparent legal exception here (that of a couple one or both of whom are below eighteen years old) is in fact no exception at all, because the issue at stake here is *precisely* that of the validity of consent.

Implications

Let us take seriously the idea that the couple themselves are not or not only the ministers of this sacrament, but are rather submitting themselves to God's ministry in the bringing of each of them into a marriage. What follows from this? It is, after all, to God's love and care that we might look for words of hope to meet the needs of those married couples who are struggling to find meaning in the context of an apparently inescapable bond. Here too we may hope to find the sense, if any can be found, of the words 'that which God has joined' as it appears related in our modern marriage services to each particular couple.

What stands *against* the very asking of the question in this way, with its reference to God's care and concern, is the perfectly natural response that marriage is a mundane fact of human existence. To 'spiritualize' it in this way is perhaps to mislead people regarding its ultimate significance, perhaps to raise false expectations regarding the nature of marriage itself. It may offer too easy a solution to the problems which couples may encounter in their marriage by permitting them to just say 'obviously we just were not meant (by God) to be married.' All of these are serious possibilities to those who share the assumption of God's involvement in the making of each marriage. Obviously, the account of marriage implied will be one which, however universal we believe it to be in its application to all human marriages, is restricted in its intelligibility to those who share its presuppositions. *Most* people are not going to understand their marriages as 'God's having brought us together.'

For those who *do* understand marriage in this way, does it make any difference to the experiences of choice and choosing which a couple may go through on their way towards marriage? Let it be said immediately that a great many Christians *will* regard it as both intelligible and of fundamental importance that they offer the possibility of their marrying, and the question of who their marriage partner might be, to God. And all the normal considerations of guidance and the discernment of God's will may be worked through by them in this aspect of their lives. However, if an already married couple both *become* Christians, there is obviously no presumption that their marriage is automatically under question or suspicion. It may be that this is a recognition that marriage is completely irrelevant to their Christian lives (which appears implausible), or that they have done something which was quite within their properly human capacity, namely to bind *themselves* irrevocably into this marriage. But more in keeping with the assumption of submission to God's making of the marriage is the belief that their marriage came about under God's care and protection *even before their conversion*. This 'presumption of providence' is significant in reading at least one biblical text, that of 1 Corinthians 7. Here, Paul seeks to answer the question 'what if I have become a Christian and my partner has not?' The interpretation of the answer he gives to this question is controversial in the cases where the 'unbelieving partner' abandons the relationship—controversial because it is not finally clear whether Paul sees re-marriage of the believer as a possibility. It is clear, though, that the case where the unbelieving partner regards the spouse's conversion as no reason to leave constitutes a continuing marriage—indeed, one in which some spiritual blessing or status is imparted to the unbeliever.

Celibacy as Calling

As noted above when mentioning Matthew 19.3-12, the range of possibilities available to human beings in the arena of human sexual relationships is traditionally viewed as either marriage or celibacy. This of course raises as many questions regarding the meaning of celibacy as it does that of marriage. It would be depressingly in line with common misunderstandings of Christian teaching on human sexual being to regard celibacy as primarily *renunciation*—not as renunciation 'for the sake of the Kingdom,' in the sense of opening up new possibilities of relationship and of service, but just as a formal 'renunciation of the flesh.' There is something true in celibacy, in the relatively undifferentiated offering and making available of the self to others, which speaks powerfully of heaven. And in the intimacy and self-giving of marriage at its best we see, too, a fragment of heavenly possibility.

The claim here will simply be this: that it makes no sense to talk of an individual's vocation *either* to marriage *or* to celibacy which makes no reference to others. The vocation to celibacy is a kind of universal vocation (making reference to availability for *all* others as the Lord may give opportunity), whilst the vocation to marriage is a special vocation to some one individual in differentiation from all others for the co-duration of their earthly existence. I am not called to marry, and then somehow left free to marry whoever I will. Nor am I called to be married, and *then*, as a second, separate act, called to marry some particular person. Admittedly, the latter may well be how the matter 'feels' to someone who has worked through the possibility of a vocation to a celibate life and has come to believe this not to be his or her calling. If, after all, I am not called to be celibate, and the alternative state is marriage, I am in a third, provisional state of being 'not yet married,' and the only question which remains is to whom I will be joined in marriage. To the status of being 'not yet married' we shall return.

Vocation and Choice

Some of the issues raised by this kind of approach are of an abstract kind. But the ones which may worry us most immediately are quite concrete and practical. Discussion of 'vocation' carries with it a commitment to a vocabulary which we have already used once, of discernment and guidance, and even to imply that there might be a sense in which from this perspective marriages might be regarded as 'arranged.' That is indeed one part of what is being suggested. The best human model we have for marriage from this perspective probably *is* the arranged marriage.

That is not at all to say, though, that this need be the appropriate or only model for practical *selection* of a marriage partner. But we would do well to recognize the mess and human misery which may result from the alternatives when we call to mind too quickly the abuses and errors and impositions which seem to be the most obvious arguments *against* a culture of 'arranged' marriages. Certainly, there may be good reason to say that a couple are better making their own decision, rather than having others to blame! But even such a view may betray a tragically static conception of the particular marriage, a view which is clearly not simply non-Christian but anti-Christian. The word 'consent' in our wedding services is a happy survivor of a picture of marriage which contrasts with the expectations of most participants.

For, in spite of our comments at the start of this chapter, it seems almost inevitable that the couple *will* understand their action in marrying as a *choice*. The hint that rather than choosing marriage it is somehow chosen *for* me, that I am called *to* this marriage, implies a profound reversal of expectation, and an attack on the idea that a marriage is constituted by the happy coincidence of the agreement of two individuals (for the moment, at least, until they change their minds) in their choices. If it *is* two choices (if *even*, we might say, two consents) that make a marriage, then where—apart from the societal concerns and the welfare of children mentioned earlier—should we look for a justification of the claims to marital permanence? Why prefer marriage to more casual forms of relationship? Marriage is *not* made by consent alone, however, for all that consent is an essential *component* in the making of any marriage. The wedding service, for example, where that consent is normally definitively expressed, is simply one event in the context of a lifelong journey. And the consent is a consenting to undergo that journey—a journey anticipating the making of many unexpected discoveries, concerning self, and spouse, and an absolutely concrete relationship which transcends the individualities of each. To a fuller investigation of this aspect of our theme we now turn.

3
Marriage and Transformation: Becoming 'One Flesh'

One quite frequently hears the matter of change, in the relationship or in a partner, cited as a reason for the collapse of a marriage. 'We grew apart'; 'he is not how he used to be.' A host of reasons may be offered which give voice to a sense of loss, a belief that the marriage has broken down, in effect that it has died. To people who feel this way about their relationship, it is almost certainly not *helpful* to be told that Christianity regards marriage as necessarily lifelong and that their vows should be enough to bind them to getting on with the graft of being married. For what continues after these words are spoken is, often enough, scarcely able to function as a marriage. Even if neither partner intends remarriage in the near future, it may appear more honest to declare the marriage over.

Vocation and Change

What is *wrong* with this has begun already in the attitude towards change, and it is here that Christians can surely make their experience tell. For if to be a Christian teaches a person anything, it is that change is not unusual but absolutely normal and something to be expected in the course of our lives lived in relationship with Christ. To preach the gospel, simply to share in any expression of our faith, is to express the urgent need to change—to repent, of course, but also to be made holy, to let go of things which hold us back in our walk of faith and to grow in the fruit of a life lived in the Spirit. If change is a fact of the Christian life, and if the gospel of Christ is of relevance to all people, then no Christian understanding of marriage can afford to ignore it.

There is, in particular, no possibility of any Christian understanding of marriage which *both* (1) takes seriously the desirability of a real depth of personal significance in the relationship of husband and wife, and also (2) rejects the necessity of personal transformation. The reason that both of these matters need to be mentioned is that someone might seek to overcome the strains of personal change upon a marriage by adopting a very minimal conception of the content of the marriage relationship. On such a view the more functional and formal the perceived rôles and duties of the couple, and the lower their expectations of the relationship into which they have entered, the better! It is not really a view which is likely to commend itself to anyone who cares for the teaching on the goods of marriage as traditionally expounded in Christian writings, because it severely undervalues both the 'iconic' and the 'relational' goods.

So we shall need to be prepared to accept as an element of our account something which is bound to be explicit in any *Christian* conception of marriage, that of change and transformation. This connects importantly with the rejection of any conception of marriage as a kind of continuing 'voluntary free association' of two individuals, in favour of the image of 'one flesh,' a form of human existence which is both *more than* and *other than* the two people who enter into it. Voluntary free association is not compatible with a view of marriage as a life-long partnership. If it were based on a continuing choice it could presumably be terminated by a withdrawal of that choice as soon as the couple 'grow apart.'

Defective Vows?

This is not particularly to assume that the vows as such play a central rôle in the inviolability of the marriage, though the language of much 'traditional' teaching on marriage may encourage such a view. Where such traditional teaching is respected it may become essential, if the ending of a 'marriage' appears desirable, to examine and prove some defect in the vows, thereby proving that there was in fact no marriage at all. There are two problems such an investigation.

Firstly, it is open to abuse because of the claims which one or both of the couple may make about their 'private intentions' or 'personal understandings' of the vows which they made. If, for example, I want to escape from a marriage, I may simply say that I never really intended the vows (that I was effectively lying), or that I did not understand the vows in the same way that they are interpreted by the authorities. To this one might respond either by saying that the vow really *was* made, in that it was correctly spoken in the correct context, and that the person who made it is thus *really* bound by it for the rest of his life or until the death of the marriage partner. That is the line taken by most on the 'vow-rigorist' side of the discussion. Or one might capitulate instantly and say that as no-one else is in a position to know what the person *privately* intended, he or she must be permitted to provide the only definitive evidence that the marriage is null and void due to this defect of intention. Intermediate positions are taken from time to time, but it is hard to see how they could be defended.

Secondly, though, and more significantly, there is a problem with the vows precisely because the person making them is unaware of what is being vowed. This unawareness operates at least two levels: that of the specific content of the lives of the couple in the marriage (as, for example, the unexpected period of unemployment, the accident or illness, or whatever), on the one hand; and that of the generalized experience of being a good lover (good husband, good wife) in marriage, on the other. To the first of these we might say that the marriage vows do their *best* to promote a sense of 'what if?' in the couple, and good marriage preparation may extend this further.[8] However, there must be some limit to the conceivability of even future *likelihoods* on the part of the couple, let alone remote possibilities. 'It will not happen to us' runs very deep in our psyche.

8 By asking, for example, whether the prospects of the marriage through financial hardship, or the illness of an elderly relative, or the possibility of infertility, have been seriously faced up to.

Joys and Hardships

In the case of what I have called the 'experience of being a good lover' (to which we might add 'the experience of allowing oneself to be loved well'), the meaning is simply this: that in actually being married one is simply not capable of knowing what it is one is promising to be willing either to be or to do. And if one *did* know, one might well hold back from making the promise on the grounds of that anticipation! The elderly couple who have learnt through both joys and hardships to share in every aspect of their lives might still, if they were honest, say that they would not have made the vows at the time, had they been able to anticipate what the marriage vows really *meant* for them. And yet also, quite without paradox, they might claim that they regarded every aspect of the history of their marriage as worthwhile for the sake of the relationship which has been built through it. Would I have *promised* to love in all circumstances and all eventualities if I had known how hard this is in practice, and what specific tests and trials awaited that promise? Probably not—yet I have become profoundly glad that I *did* make that promise, and am committed to its fulfilment.

It might be worth adding that whilst illness and unemployment and other such hardships are the most obvious forms of strain which might be dreaded in a marriage, the attempted sharing of joys and of health too can bring their unexpected pressures. We are not perhaps all that good at sharing pleasure. Even in the sharing of parenthood, rivalries for affection might ruin a relationship where there is no apparent cause of 'hardship' to begin with. Attempting to share in material prosperity might bring jealousies and other traumas to a relationship which would actually cope quite well with poverty! What the marriage vows ask us to promise is, in effect, to be a good lover to the partner in *all* things, and this is something to which it is much easier to aspire than to promise. Those who perhaps know themselves too well may feel the vows as a burden most keenly. Others, more careless of their words, may scarcely notice the vows at all.

Open to the Future

There is a kind of critique implicit within Christianity of any of the simpler and more obvious kinds of response to the question 'why did you marry him/her?' Whether the response is couched in terms of what my partner was *like* when I married, or what (perhaps under consciously or unconsciously anticipated manipulation by self or in-laws, or...) he or she might *become*, the transformation which *counts* is the one to which Christ calls us. Expressed at its most abstract, perhaps for humour's sake but also to make the point, I may not have wanted to be married to an especially holy person—but then, that was a sign of my own need to grow in holiness, too!

Each marriage thus takes into itself the possibility of personal transformation. This means that the couple themselves should be aware of marriage as a vocation oriented towards a future and a quality of relationship which they are perhaps to a very large degree unable to predict. This might well offer a better reading of the consent than anything we have thus far seen. To what do I give my consent? To whatever this relationship may become; to the open-ended future which offers itself to us. To at least open up the possibility of reading consent in *this* way is to remind the couple that they may face many events in their lives which are outside their immediate control, but which they may genuinely face, and through which they will grow both in themselves and in their marriage. (After all, in the case of a marriage which finds its human origins in romantic affection it may often be that the couple are each quite unknown to the other, hidden behind a construction of fantasy. Here the first problem may well be to discard my perceptions about who it is I have married, so that I can come to appreciate the truth more fully.)

A parallel may help us here, and it may be worth relating the above reflections to language used of the Kingdom of God. We are aware as we read the New Testament of three kinds of temporal language relating to the Kingdom. It is present as something which has been inaugurated in Christ, is growing in human history and yet is also still to come. This language of the complete, the coming to be and the yet to be attained are of great significance for marriage. To get married is to *look forward* to being married, a looking forward which will still not quite have been exhausted after over sixty years of marriage, whilst it is also already to have taken part in the bringing into being of something which has been 'marked off' from the rest of society as a completed marrying. And this expectation challenges the view that the goal of marriage preparation is to achieve a stable relationship which external threats will not overwhelm. The relationship *must* change, but that change is part of the nature of being married, part of the process of becoming 'one flesh.'

Cohabitation and Vocation

In essence, then, this is the point where cohabitation and marriage most obviously show themselves as distinct. One must be careful about this, because cohabiting couples might well plan their relationship to be for life, and simply have rejected a *wedding rite*, precisely because it has been tainted by the failure of those who offer it (church and state) to support and nurture marriages by teaching and practical help. Such a judgment on the churches appears harsh, but viewed from the outside might not seem unreasonable. However, where cohabitation is designed as a means of providing for a stable partnership along with ready means of escape for either partner, it is clearly and consciously failing to fulfil the vision of marriage outlined in these pages. The uncomfortable additional fact is that as long as the practical experience of a great many of the marriages in our society is that of a premature end in divorce, those who choose cohabitation rather than marriage are behaving entirely rationally.

They are behaving rationally *first of all* because they are unlikely to see any significant difference between their relationship and a marriage which stands every chance of ending in divorce. (And if there is a difference, it may be in the cohabiting couple's greater honesty in refusing to make the vows.) And they are behaving rationally *secondly* in that they may simply fail to see beyond the limited possibilities for human relationships which their experience has taught them and their society encourages them to believe in. In a political economy which relies on and responds to the desire for fairly immediate personal gratification, and in which insecurity in employment and housing are very real, the likelihood of individuals seeing any good in sincere commitment to a lifelong relationship, carrying with it an open-ended acceptance of whatever life may bring, is remote—remote, though not absolutely impossible.

One response to this might be to claim that it is much too bleak; many couples, after all, do still desire marriage. This is true enough, though we should be wary of assuming that they have accepted the kind of vision of marriage which will enable the sustaining of them in that relationship throughout their lives. One kind of case would be a couple who regard lifelong marriage as a romantic dream, something to hope for which just *might* be true for them. They accept that some marriages end in divorce—accept indeed that *theirs* might. They *hope* that it will not, but they have little idea even in the most general sense of the open kind of personal commitment which they would need to make in order to build their relationship as a marriage. The second kind of case is that of a couple who accept (along with the politicians and sociologists who recognize the importance of the traditional family) that their marriage—their *being married*—may be a source of stability in the nurture of their children. The *point* of their being married may well come under scrutiny once the children have reached a certain age, not simply because in the years of child care they have exhausted that which they had in common, but perhaps even because the nurture of children was actually the sole basis of their marriage in the first place.

So in a perverse sense one might *almost* welcome the rise in cohabitation, for the way in which it forces attention back on to the positive, primary internal goods of marriage and allows for the presentation of a genuine human good which, if it is rejected, is at least rejected with greater understanding. Unless marriage is both understood and seen to be valuable, people will reject it. The challenge is both to teach, and to set an example. In our teaching, we may do well to claim boldly that marriage can never be 'provisional,' *at least in the sense that one might survive within it whilst waiting for someone or something better to come along.*[9] If one cannot 'try out' Christianity to see if it suits one before accepting Christ, so too one cannot 'try out' marriage. The sense of provisionality implicit in the trying itself threatens the complete undermining of the very thing which is claimed to be undergoing trial.[10]

9 In the sense that no particular marriage is ever 'completed,' of course, it may be right to regard there as being at least one sense in which marriage *is* 'provisional.' For while marriage may be ended at death, it appears implausible to think that it could be perfected to the point where further discovery and growth were no longer possible during earthly life.

10 The couple who cohabit as a 'test' of their potential marriage relationship *as such*, seeing their

4
The Difference it Makes

It is time to draw together some of the practical implications of viewing marriage as vocation, as a calling of two people to a union of life in which God acts to bring about their joining. The first might be to ask what difference it makes in the finding of a marriage partner. The ways in which couples first meet are obviously very varied—through the 'singles' column of the newspaper, the enmity at work which turns to deeper understanding and to love, the manipulations of 'you ought to meet...' by friends or relatives. And nothing that is said here rules any of them out of account in advance. We might, though, be properly worried about (for example) a wedding to a previously unknown partner as a prize in a game show. The problem in this last case is as much the apparent frivolity of the occasion (which is unlikely to foster genuine reflection and consent) as the method of selecting a partner. If the selection were done with the kind of care and concern which parents might seek to provide in the arrangement of marriage partners for their offspring, there might from *that* perspective at least be little to quarrel with.

Vocation and Authority

My greatest fear in the conception of marriage as spiritual vocation is to open up for the more avowedly authoritarian leaderships of our churches a new avenue of potentially ill-considered imposition upon their flocks. It is worth reminding ourselves that where marriages are 'arranged' a burden of discernment of almost incredible weight is placed upon those with the responsibility to choose. (I may speak here at a purely human level, and think of parents hoping for no more than a tolerable life for their offspring.) We might do well, however, to remember that in a sense *all* those who participate approvingly in our wedding services are in the position of 'sponsors' of the marriage, and so supporters of it. If we believe the marriage right, we are to some degree responsible for it.

However the couple come to marriage, it is important that at the point of marrying they should be able to submit their futures as individuals to the vocation they will share as a couple. This is inevitably bound to be expressed in different terms to a couple who are not Christians, but the idea should be intelligible enough to them (and may, sadly, put many off marriage at all). From a *Christian* couple, if the distinction may be clearly drawn, one might almost hope for a similar declaration to that required of a minister in the Church of England

---

cohabiting relationship as a '*trial* marriage' from which they may escape if it does not 'work,' have simply failed to comprehend the fundamental difference between a marriage and a free association. Their cohabitation is so different in character from marriage that it can hardly be a test or a preparation for it.

at ordination: 'Do you believe that God is calling you to...?' The advantages of such a declaration would lie in the reminder that the marriage transcends the sum of their consents, and is something into which they will grow as their relationship is explored and developed. It is not something which they can simply make in their own power. It serves as a reminder that they are not in absolute control of all that life might bring to them, and that their marrying is not simply a giving up of the claims they have on their own lives as individuals, or a gaining of rights over the other, but a coming into existence of something quite new. And it also serves as a reminder of the source of the help, guidance and encouragement which they will need.

Haste or Delay?

To this extent we might want to suggest that, just as a couple might marry too quickly, maybe quite overwhelmed by a sudden romance, and so fail to count the actual 'cost' of marriage in the giving up of claims to self, so also couples might actually delay marriage too long. The significance of the belief and decision that I should be this person's marriage partner for life is sufficient to make some reflection appropriate. But much of the cause for delay in marrying might just be a failure to appreciate that a marriage cannot be completed in advance of its coming into being. Once the couple are sufficiently convinced that their relationship is right, there seems no general reason to delay the kind of learning and growing which can take place *within* marriage. Many marriages are perhaps damaged by delay as much as by haste. The couple might wait for the stable maturity of each of them as individuals, when learning to change together would serve them better. 'Waiting for marriage' can have its place, and will be inevitable for many couples, but if what is waited for is an end of change and personal growth then the threat is of a wait in vain, and perhaps of a false understanding of the nature of marriage too.

The false understanding is one which has been our target throughout this booklet. Marriage is *not* a relationship which at its best is changeless; it is *not* a relationship to which the couple may give as little of themselves as they choose. The marriage is the whole of both of them, and to the extent that they fail to be sensitive and open to the possibility of sharing in the whole of their lives, serving and communicating with the other in the whole of their beings, the marriage is less than 'one flesh.' On the other hand, such a sharing will not come easily. This sharing, this transparency of each to the other, is the work of many years and is likely to be the fruit of learning through many apparent failures. The good news about marriage is that it is possible and that the good to human beings which comes through it can be very great.

Expectations of Vocation

We may expect too little of marriage, may fail to desire the goods which it can bring. Can we expect too much? Perhaps we can, in the sense that we might despair prematurely of failures which are actually the gateway to success—the romantic vision of marriage as something which just 'happens *to*' us, rather than something we live and grow into. It is not that the aspirations for 'success' are wrong. No-one should easily be *content* with a marriage which by the standards of the primary 'goods' referred to above is a failure. Marriage, the couple may need to be reminded, lies *ahead* as well as in the present and the past.

They may need to be *reminded* of this. To a couple who are finding marriage hard going, and tragically almost *especially* to a Christian couple who are finding marriage hard going, reminders may be few and far between. This is not least because anything which looks like an admission of failure may be very hard to make, where divorce is regarded as anathema. And where divorce is *not* regarded as anathema they may find little *support* for the continuing of their marriage anyway, if they have hit upon problems! What is needed, then, is something very akin to *spiritual direction* for marriages—perhaps the pairing of young couples with older ones, perhaps the offering of guidance from a celibate man or woman who has in the offering of himself or herself to many others learnt much about growth and change in relationships. Above all, something is needed which respects the *particularity* of each marriage, and the growth and nurture appropriate to it. Books, techniques and formulae which may be very helpful to many could disturb or mislead others.

Grace and Presumption

Should such reflections appear as a claim of the all-sufficiency of God's grace, in whatever form it might be offered (as strength to forebear, or imputation of a will to change, or in some other way) to such an extent that no marriage is beyond salvation? Helen Oppenheimer criticizes such language, which may reflect criticism of a claim actually made on a number of occasions in P T Forsyth's work on marriage.[11] It is tempting to suggest that the issue here is one of presuming too much or too little of God's grace, and that if this is so one had better choose to presume too much. The point for anyone wishing to assimilate marriage to sacramental theology, though, a subject mentioned all too briefly earlier on, is somewhat different. Can our *presumption* of the availability of grace ever cause us to run astray from the specific details of God's will? Can it lead us to believe in God's personal gracious commitment to the support of a marriage which he does not in fact desire?

Our 'presumption of providence' is the best guide we have to the question 'which marriages does God will?' One simple answer is that we *presume* this to be true of all actual, legally valid human marriages.[12] For some people, this *presumption* is elevated to the status of a *universal truth* that all 'actually existing

11 Peter Taylor Forsyth, *Marriage—Its Ethics and Religion* (London: Hodder and Stoughton, nd [1912]) p 39f; Helen Oppenheimer, *Marriage* (note 7 above), pp 62-64.
12 This might require some qualification, but appears basically correct.

marriages' are willed by God. Others might believe that some marriages may even *come into being* out of the hardness of human hearts, and that the permissibility of divorce relies on our capacity to discern those marriages which continue to demonstrate such hardness of heart. Yet holders of either position might say that the reality includes—and surely, the reality *does* in fact include—the premature ending and rejection of good marriages in divorce, with a motivation driven from despair rather than hope. And the very *absence of hope* is enough for us to see here (albeit perhaps unconsciously) a turning away from God.

One problem may well be to understand what characteristics we look for in order to discern whether something really *counts as a marriage*—one aspect of the debates over the nature and status of cohabitation. Insofar as cohabitation is a positive rejection of marriage, a failure of the individuals to submit themselves to something new and irrevocable to which the biblical image of 'one flesh' points, it seems hard to recognize such relationships as significantly related to the view of marriage taken here at all. In fact, it appears to be one more form of assertion of the immediate self and its self-understanding over any higher calling which might claim it, a characterization which is remarkably close to a great deal of Christian understanding of sin.

'Not Yet Married...'

Brief mention needs to be made of the status of being 'not yet married.' This is important because the restriction of categories to 'celibate' and 'married' is patently false to the current experience of a great many people, who simply do not know whether between now and their deaths they will be married or not. Many may have *expectations*, whether of marriage or not, and it is important to remember that one may be 'not *yet* married' as much in one's eighties as at eighteen, and even perhaps be just as open to the possibility of marriage. It is significant and important that there is increasing attention to the place of the single person in the Christian community. It is significant for the support which it may offer to individuals perplexed by the pressures to deny the possibility of deeper fulfilment in human relationships in favour of the relatively or absolutely casual sexual encounter; and significant also for the rôle which the not-yet-married may offer in the support of marriages. This support is seen effectively not just in their respect for actually existing marriages, but also in the forms of waiting, seeking and testing of their *own* callings which they are willing to countenance and submit to.

Redemption and Relationships

To three groups of people it is particularly important to address a word at the end of this essay, and the word is in essence the same to all. It is that God can bring redemption even to the situation you find yourself in. The first group is those who are finding difficulty in their marriages. The second is those who have been divorced. And the third is those who believe that they have missed their opportunity to marry.

To the first group the only word to be spoken is a simple restatement of the offer of redemption—of the committing of the situation to God, and to the offer of power in patience, healing and transformation which he can bring. To the second group, those who are divorced and are wondering what future there might be for them, there is no 'general' answer, but the reassurance that the God who has taken, remade and used broken lives in the past offers that same possibility to you, to work through and put the past behind you and to look forward in hope. The specific human *content* to which that life of hope may lead is quite beyond generalized predictions, even and perhaps especially regarding the question of future marriage.

There may be those who feel that they have missed or rejected an opportunity for marriage which was provided by God, and that their life is, as a result, fundamentally estranged from God's plan for them. Such a feeling of estrangement—which is, of course, by no means restricted to the area of marriage—can be met by a number of responses. It may be that the feeling of having missed God's calling is actually a failure to acknowledge personal regret at the loss of a past relationship, that is, that it bears no content of genuine spiritual discernment at all, but is simply a failure to 'let go.' On the other hand, it may be a genuine feeling that the individual was not open to doing God's will. We might then be agnostic about what God actually *did* expect of him or her in relation to the apparent opportunity and yet still feel that this admitted unwillingness alone is an appropriate occasion for repentance.

In the case of an individual who wants to say 'It is all hopeless. I have missed God's path for my life' we need to say quite firmly that the God who forgives can also make new beginnings and open new opportunities. Controversially, one might also suggest that God is aware, in advance of our ever rejecting his direction, that we *will* reject it. We certainly sin, but he knows in advance that we will, and his fundamental call upon our lives, that we acknowledge his lordship and have faith in him, allows us to trust that a new beginning is ever available. From the standpoint of the repentant sinner, the past may appear to be so many broken and rejected opportunities. From the standpoint of the forgiven sinner it may appear that God's grace has opened up the possibility of a new life fashioned from the ruins of the past. There is no meaningful sense in which God's will can be *ultimately* overcome. For all the truth that there are any number of ways in which we may rebel from the patterns of life which are intended for us, the resurrection is a powerful reassurance that our faith is never in vain, and that we never have to live without hope.

The Possibility of Joy

There may be an altogether too serious view of marriage—one hopes that this booklet may not have contributed to the furtherance of it!—which places it quite above human possibility and, whether for the magnitude of decision or the incapacity of the person, encourages the replacement of it in human life by something else. That 'something else' might be a shadowy substitute for marriage, or a mocking contempt for it, or even, just possibly at times, a life of sexual renunciation perceived negatively, not as positive celibacy but as a rejection of sexual being. When we say that marriage is 'not to be undertaken lightly,' we must not allow those words to conjure up a series of excuses to undermine the proper place of marriage in human life.

Christians surely *do* have a *serious* word to speak on the place and nature of marriage in human life. Yet, firstly, we may add that the concept of *joy* is also a crucial one for Christians. If marriage is all we may believe it to be, it may well be a source of the superficial joys of fun and all the profounder joys of remembered and anticipated pleasures which a perfect trust permits. Trust, in fact, is very much to the point. Pity those couples who are unable to trust, not simply in each other, but in a future hope which lies not simply in their own hands but also in that of their maker. And this, then, is the second response to the claim of over-seriousness. If we can live in perfect trust, we need not fear or worry, but can *expect* our marriages to grow in love and unity, to be truly *good*, sources of well-being for their participants and also for the society in which they are placed. Marriage may become a discovering in which the call to be childlike will make sense even to those who do not yet know Christ for themselves, and in which the levity of play and the deepest seriousness and commitment of play may also be found.

The demand of seriousness and sobriety should not lead people to delay marriage where it is right. If the goods of marriage are such as they have traditionally been held to be by Christians, then the low esteem into which marriage has fallen ought to worry us not simply out of concern for social cohesion but for the dishonour afforded to our creator. It is not enough simply to regret the rise of alternatives to marriage. The positive task of promoting the goods which marriage can bring belongs not merely to the teaching of the pulpit and the academy, but to the lives of each and every Christian, whether married, celibate, or, indeed, not-yet-married.